POCKET STUDY SKILLS

Series Editor: **Kate Williams**,
Oxford Brookes University, UK

For the time-pushed student, the *Pocket Study Skills* pack a lot of advice into a little book. Each guide focuses on a single crucial aspect of study giving you step-by-step guidance, handy tips and clear advice on how to approach the important areas which will continually be at the core of your study ethic.

Published

Blogs, Wikis, Podcasts and More   *Andy Pulman*

Brilliant Writing Tips for Students   *Julia Copus*

Getting Critical   *Kate Williams*

Planning Your Essay   *Janet Godwin*

Referencing and Understanding Plagiarism
    Kate Williams and Jude Carroll

Science Study Skills   *Sue Robbins*

Further titles are planned

Pocket Study Skills
Series Standing Order
ISBN 978-0230-21605-1
(outside North America only)

You can receive future titles in this series as they are published by placing a standing order. Please contact your bookseller or, in case of difficulty, write to us at the address below with your name and address, the title of the series and the ISBN quoted above.

Customer Services Department, Macmillan Distribution Ltd Houndmills, Basingstoke, Hampshire RG21 6XS England

POCKET STUDY SKILLS
Andy Pulman

BLOGS
WIKIS
PODCASTS
& MORE

palgrave
macmillan

First published 2009 by
PALGRAVE MACMILLAN

Palgrave Macmillan in the UK is an imprint of Macmillan Publishers Limited, registered in England, company number 785998, of Houndmills, Basingstoke, Hampshire RG21 6XS.

Palgrave Macmillan in the US is a division of St Martin's Press LLC, 175 Fifth Avenue, New York, NY 10010.

Palgrave Macmillan is the global academic imprint of the above companies and has companies and representatives throughout the world.

Palgrave® and Macmillan® are registered trademarks in the United States, the United Kingdom, Europe and other countries

ISBN-13: 978-0-230-22391-2

This book is printed on paper suitable for recycling and made from fully managed and sustained forest sources. Logging, pulping and manufacturing processes are expected to conform to the environmental regulations of the country of origin.

A catalogue record for this book is available from the British Library.

A catalog record is available from the Library of Congress.

10 9 8 7 6 5 4 3 2 1
18 17 16 15 14 13 12 11 10 09

Printed in China

Contents

Acknowledgements

Thank you, to: Julia (for her love, encouragement and support), Kate (for editorial guidance), Suzannah (for concept approval), Sallie (for illustrations) and Caroline (for editorial consultancy). Thanks also go to Mum, Sue and of course Gellie – and YOU for buying it (!).

Introduction

Welcome to this essential guide to the world of blogs, wikis, podcasts and much more. These terms may currently seem like another world to you, but once you've had a chance to read through this guide you should be able to impress your friends, family and tutors with your grasp of a new range of technologies and how you can best use them to help improve your study skills.

Palgrave Pocket Study Skills have been designed for your pocket (or handbag) so that you can take them with you anywhere. You can use this guide at home, on the move, in university or even in the bath (if so, careful you don't drop it).

As a guide it's been written to provide you with a resource that you can dip into, as you need, for reference and for those moments when you need inspiration or guidance. There's also a glossary of useful terms at the back of the book for when you need to quickly find a definition and aren't near a computer (the first use of a term explained in the glossary appears in **bold**).

Throughout the book there are useful examples for you to follow or ideas to try. If you have time it could be helpful to visit some of the websites mentioned or try out a couple of the exercises suggested but it's not essential or required.

The worlds of technology and education are constantly changing – consider this your friendly guide to helping you on the road to understanding how the web and study skills are linked together and how they can help you to do what you want quickly and easily, without stress.

Happy reading, and above all – good studying.

Andy Pulman

1 What is the internet, anyway?

The internet connects computers all over the world.

It allows information to be transmitted immediately, and collaboration and interaction between individuals and their computers to take place without worrying about location or time differences.

In 1999, Tim Berners-Lee, the pioneer of the World Wide Web (**WWW**), described his vision of the Web as:

> **'Encompassing the decentralised organic growth of ideas, technology, and society.'**

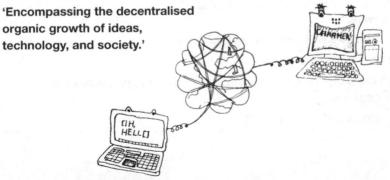

How does the internet work?

Each page on the internet is known by an internet address (called a Uniform Resource Locator or **URL** for short). The URL is the address that specifies the location of a file on the internet. It identifies the location of any website, in the same way that your home address is used when someone sends you a letter. A URL looks like this: http://www.mywebsite.co.uk

The internet is accessed with software called **browsers**. A browser is a piece of software that allows you to view a webpage on the internet (popular browsers include Firefox, Flock, Internet Explorer and Safari).

Web browsers

Firefox: http://www.mozilla.com/en-US/firefox/

Flock: http://flock.com/

Internet Explorer: http://www.microsoft.com/windows/products/winfamily/ie/default.mspx

Safari: http://www.apple.com/safari/

Collaborative communities and Web 2.0

In the early days of the internet, information was edited and published by few and read by many, but this has changed in the last few years.

The term Web 2.0 refers to a second generation of web-based communities and services (such as social networking, **wikis** and **blogs**) that aim to help creativity, collaboration and sharing.

You and Web 2.0

Have you ever used Wikipedia, Facebook, Bebo, Flickr, YouTube or MySpace?

Congratulations! You are already part of the Web 2.0 revolution.

Web 2.0 facts: a web of trust

In 2009, OFCOM (Office of Communications) noted that:

- 17% of adults talk to people they don't know on social networking sites.
- 44% of adults leave their privacy settings open so their profiles are viewable by anybody.

Whilst offering tremendous potential, Web 2.0 also presents opportunities for people to use the information available on the internet for unscrupulous purposes such as identity fraud and theft.

Web 2.0 safety checklist

Check whether you have protected yourself:

Action	Checklist
Don't give out personal information in a public profile.	
Know where you're posting – make sure you know which posts will be made public and which are only viewable by friends.	
Alter your privacy setting so that you don't leave your profile open by default.	
Don't assume others are always telling the truth.	
Never agree to meet an otherwise unknown social networking friend in person.	
Go and meet your friends for real every now and then. They won't bite!	

Information literacy

The world of technology is in a constant state of flux. You have access to a wide range of different resources with information made available to you in many different locations and formats. Books, magazines, newspapers, television, CDs, DVDs, mobile phones, **MP3** players and the internet all offer you a huge choice.

'Information literacy' is defined by CILIP (2009) as:

'Knowing when and why you need information, where to find it, and how to evaluate, use and communicate it in an ethical manner.'

Are you information literate?

Think about a question that needs answering:

- Where was Charles Darwin born?
- What is the best-selling single of all time in the UK?
- Can penguins fly?

Where do you go for the answer?	
How do you go about locating the answer?	
How do you recognise when you have an answer?	
How do you communicate this information?	
How do you organise it?	
How do you apply it?	

Assess your level

SCONUL (2009) identified various skills for information literacy and five levels of competency (your ability to perform skills):

1 Novice   4 Proficient
2 Absolute beginner   5 Expert
3 Competent

What level do you consider yourself to be at?

Finding your level helps assess your strengths and weaknesses – you might find you are better than you originally thought!

Thinking about the question you asked a minute ago, rate your ability using the SCONUL competency rating.

Where do you go for the answer?	(e.g. I am an **Expert** at knowing where to find an answer)
How do you go about locating the answer?	
How do you recognise when you have an answer?	
How do you communicate this information?	
How do you organise it?	
How do you apply it?	

The digital revolution

The good

The digital revolution – where information is converted into thin air and transmitted around the world – is transforming industries and provides opportunities and challenges for our world.

The 'knowledge economy' is seen as key to ensuring economic prosperity and global access to markets. The rapid growth of the internet and mergers between technology, media and telecom companies have contributed to the birth of an 'information society.'

Like it or not, we are all a part of this society and when you study there is an expectation that you will be ready, willing and able to use technology.

The bad

Information can come at a cost, with what Shimmon (2000) described as a 'digital divide' emerging between the 'information rich' and 'information poor'.

> **Digitally divided?**
> The digital revolution raises questions of equity of access to, and use of, information. Think about what changes in technology have recently taken place.
>
> **How it affects you**
> Turn off your phone, unplug your MP3 player and switch off your computer. How would you function without your regular fix of information?
>
> **How you feel**
> How would your life be different if you had no access at all? How would you feel?

The ugly

The rise in the use of the internet also raises legal and ethical issues – like freedom and security of information, copyright and plagiarism. As you are reading this, antisocial activities are taking place on the internet.

A new identity can be easily created – how do you know that the person you are swapping information with in a chat room is who they say they are?

More worryingly, anyone can post comments about anyone else online – how do you know that the information you are reading on the internet is correct?

Identity fraud

You wouldn't hand over personal information like photos, your mobile phone number, email and personal address to a complete stranger. So think twice before you do exactly the same thing online – every time you add lots of personal information onto social networking websites.

In 2007, the UK Fraud Prevention Service (CIFAS) identified and protected 65,000 victims of identity theft (CIFAS, 2009). One of the main problems is that people don't realise the significance of the kind of information they put onto websites and who might access it.

Ethics

Ethical considerations are important for information and its use (think of it as your moral values and rules for using, viewing and sharing information). These include rights to:

- seek information (the ability to be able to look for information without problem)
- know information (held about you by others or that you hold on them)
- receive information and censorship limits (some countries limit the amount of material you can access via the internet)
- communicate information (the right to freedom of speech is different in some countries than others).

Good practice

How ethical is your use of the internet?

Have you ever downloaded music from the internet without paying?

Have you used an image you copied from the internet without obtaining permission from the copyright holder?

Have you ever emailed an embarrassing photo of a friend to someone else without asking your friend if it was OK first?

Further information

Visit the internet Detective office and read the section on good ethics:

http://www.vts.intute.ac.uk/detective/crimestoppers.html

Are you on the right side of the law? Either give yourself a gold star or go directly to jail without passing Go.

Along with 'rights' come duties and responsibilities, including:

▶ protecting others' rights through professional ethics
▶ trying to reduce the gap between the information rich and poor
▶ withholding information
▶ maintaining privacy and data protection
▶ recognising ownership rights and copyright – important for you when you study
  (e.g. crediting sources in essays and avoiding plagiarism).

Internet ethics

Choose from an illegal or antisocial activity listed below and find out more about it. Use the Glossary section to view any term you don't understand:

▶ hacking	▶ spoofing	▶ malware (malicious software)
▶ spamming	▶ virus attacks	▶ spyware (spying software)
▶ phishing	▶ identity fraud	

Protecting information

Let's go phishing

Phishers are technically competent con artists or identity thieves who use tricks like fake websites, fake emails and instant messages to trick you into divulging sensitive information, such as bank and credit card numbers (and then cleaning them out!!).

Your bank will NEVER ask you to reveal your password in an email – would you give your password to a stranger on a street who asked for it?

Think about online communication in the same way as you would a face-to-face chat and be cautious.

Freedom of information

This protects your right to know and receive any information held (unless exempted) by certain organisations. In the UK, you have the right to request information held on you by public sector organisations like government departments, the police and even universities and colleges.

Legislation giving you rights to know about information held about you in the UK comes from the Data Protection Act (1998) and the Freedom of Information Act (2000).

Copyright legislation

This is designed to protect the creator of original work from moral or economic exploitation. It prevents anyone other than the copyright owner copying, publishing, adapting or performing a work, except under special circumstances.

In your personal life you might download and copy tracks of music and give them to your friends, or select a photo you see on the internet and use it on your website. You will have infringed copyright if you have not obtained the copyright owner's permission first.

Plagiarism

This means representing someone else's work as your own or using someone else's work without acknowledgement. Examples of plagiarism are:

▸ direct importation into work of more than a single phrase from another person's work without quotation marks and identification of the source
▸ making a copy of all or part of another person's work and presenting it as your own
▸ making extensive use of another person's work, either by summarising or paraphrasing it merely by changing a few words or altering the order, without acknowledgement
▸ use of the ideas of another person without acknowledgement, or the submission

or presentation of work as your own which is substantially the ideas or intellectual data of someone else.

Plagiarism in universities is treated as a serious offence and plagiarised work can be disqualified.

It is *not* illegal.

At best it is about lack of confidence (you may need to work on your academic writing skills). It could be laziness, or last-minute panic. At worst, when a student deliberately passes off someone else's work as his or her own, it is a disciplinary offence.

You can avoid plagiarism by the correct use of referencing (see the section on Referencing in Chapter 7). See also *Referencing and Understanding Plagiarism* in this series.

More on plagiarism
The University of Leeds: Plagiarism Awareness website brings together a range of resources on reducing plagiarism:
http://www.ldu.leeds.ac.uk/plagiarism/index.php

Technology in education

The internet can be used for communication and collaboration with individuals and groups worldwide via email, discussion lists and social software tools. You might already use these in your social life. What web-based tools can you expect to use at college or university? Here are some of the most common.

Email

Email allows communication (one-to-one or one-to-many) between people on the internet. An individual has his or her own unique address – an electronic mail (or **email**) address:

astudent@university.ac.uk

Using an email account at university requires a little more thought than one you use socially (who you send to, the type of message that you send, the language you use (see **netiquette** in Chapter 3).

Discussion lists

People with a common interest can communicate together through discussion lists, which enable one-to-many communication via email.

You normally subscribe to join a discussion list and choose whether you want to receive all emails sent between list members or a digest version (received daily or weekly). This can sometimes be the best choice – if the list is popular you may find yourself receiving 20 emails a day otherwise!

Discussion forums

On a discussion forum, messages are entered into a common area (sometimes known as a conferencing area). These areas enable electronic conversations to develop by users posting new messages or responding to existing ones (known as a **discussion thread**). Software enables the threads to be followed in sequence as messages grow to form an archive of discussion. This form of communication is known as **asynchronous**.

Discussion forums can be open so that everyone can access and take part in the discussion or can be closed so that only selected people can access and participate.

Virtual Learning Environment (VLE)

A **VLE** provides a place to access different resources that you might be expected to use on your course.

You will be given a **password** and **user ID** to access your VLE and it might include a variety of elements such as discussion forums, blogs and wikis in addition to downloadable course information (unit guides, lecture notes and slides, reading lists and timetables).

VLE examples include Blackboard, WebCT and Moodle.

Netiquette is network etiquette, the do's and don'ts of online communication.

Tips for email and discussion forums

Communicating via email or in a discussion forum is very different from speaking to someone face to face. Meanings are conveyed through typed words, so you cannot see people nod their heads or laugh or frown.

Emotions can easily be misunderstood.

Remember the person at the other end – they have feelings like you do.

What you say may have a different meaning for people who can't see you. For example: 'You must be joking' without seeing a smile, or 'I don't believe you' without seeing a grimace.

Bad netiquette

The following are considered bad netiquette:

- *Shouting*: typing your emails in CAPITALS.
- *Flaming*: a flame is sent or posted to insult or complain with the intention of causing offence and provoking a response.
- *Trolling*: a troll is somebody who posts or sends with the intention of annoying someone or disrupting a discussion or environment.

Good netiquette

Always thank, acknowledge and support:

- 'Andy, I liked your comment …'
- 'I agree with Julia's idea that …'

Acknowledge before you disagree:

- 'What I think you mean is … I hope that's right? My own view differs as follows …'

Avoid very impersonal statements like:

- 'This is the way it is …'
- 'It's a fact that …'

Always include a subject line, title or header indicating the contents of your message. People see this before they see the contents and may use it to decide whether or not to read it.

Make sure your title is clear and short.

Try to make your messages brief (no longer than one or two screens if possible).

 BLOGS, WIKIS, PODCASTS AND MORE

A modern dilemma

Nathan sends an email to Amy requesting some information – how should he reply to her message?

> Nathan,
>
> I already sent you what you asked for
>
> **YOU ARE AN IDIOT IF YOU'VE LOST IT – GET A LIFE !!!!!**
>
> Amy

Try to adhere to the same standards of behaviour online that you follow in real life (as long as you're well behaved in real life too!)

Test your netiquette

Albion.com provides a good netiquette resource with tips and a quiz:

http://www.albion.com/netiquette/

Email netiquette

Sometimes taking a minute to reread what you've written before sending an email makes all the difference.

Email 'think before you send it' checklist:

Action	Checklist
Is the tone of your email ok? Is it too casual or vague? If so, amend it.	
Are there insults, swearing or offensive terms in your email? Remove them.	
Would you say the contents of the email to the person's face? If not, rewrite it.	
Could I not just speak to the person (by phone or in person) rather than sending it? If yes, don't send it.	
Would I be happy to receive this email if someone sent it to me?	

Flames and trolls

Choosing how to deal with a flame or troll can be difficult as the wrong approach could lead to further trouble. Your options are:

1 **Ignore it**: Usually the best method is to ignore trouble, as tutors will normally step in. Ignoring a troll is almost always the best approach as if nobody responds, the troller will get bored and go away. Users will sometimes add a warning: *Do not feed the troll* (**DNFTT**).

2 **Respond rationally**: This can make the flamer look irrational but a troll can be a direct challenge to authority so they are difficult to ignore. A reference to an earlier posting answering the troll's points can be a good way of defusing a situation.

3 **Flame back**: It is usually a bad idea to respond back in this way as it only shows your own suitability for trolling or being flamed in the future. Flaming back also provokes the flamer into responding again.

4 **Explain**: If you can remain calm, you could try to respond with an explanation. You could reply to a flamer indicating they may have misunderstood what you said, and give a more detailed explanation in your reply.

Email chain letters and other irritations

Why do people forward chain letters? Don't open an email if you don't recognise the author, especially if it has an attachment, which might be a virus. Think twice before forwarding any email or opening suspect attachments.

If it does not say, 'this is a chain letter' that doesn't mean it's *not* a chain letter. We are all guilty of occasionally forwarding suspect emails. Try to think before you do.

Spam, spam and more spam

Do not respond to a 'remove' facility provided by a spam email – it's a trick to get you to confirm your **email address** as a valid one to which they might send you more spam emails. Delete it from your inbox and also delete it from your deleted items folder if you have one.

Forwarding correctly

There are many email hoaxes, which will probably never die because it is too easy to forward items on to others. With email it is very easy to 'reply to all' without thinking about who will be receiving it.

It is always worth looking at who the email you are forwarding on has been sent to and who you are forwarding it on to. Always check the 'To' and 'CC' boxes before you send an email (especially if the content of your email is private and confidential).

And, if you decide that you must forward an email or funny cat picture, use **BCC** ('blind copy') and remove any previously forwarded email addresses, so you don't share and publicise all of the correspondents' email addresses with a list of people they don't know. With a blind copy, recipients only see their own email address.

BUT remember good netiquette advice: never forward an email without the sender's permission!

Whoever you forward an email to might forward it to someone else, so always be sure that what you send you would be happy for others to see.

4   Beautiful and beastly blogs

What is a blog?

A blog is a method of publishing information online, similar to keeping a journal and writing entries. A blog can provide a continuous up-to-date view of somebody's work, ideas, activities, progress, development or whatever they are interested in talking about.

Blog origins

Blog is a shortened version of the term 'weblog':

~~we~~**blog**

Entries, known as **posts**, are normally short in length and are added regularly. Each new post is added to the top of the first page, with the most recent entries shown below. Older entries are archived on previous pages.

An example blog:

Visit http://andyp.edublogs.org/ to view my personal blog.

Look at the screen layout and see how the most recent entry is displayed at the top of the page.

Who writes blogs?

A blog usually belongs to a single person, but multiple **blogger**s can also contribute to one blog. They can be run by individuals, groups, institutions or corporations, and cover areas as diverse as politics and commerce, professional and personal interests, and education.

Traditionally, journals have been private or secret affairs, and were never linked to other journals. Blogs, by contrast, are social in nature, encapsulating the ethos of Web 2.0, whether open to the whole world or only visible to a small group of friends.

Microblogs and tumblelogs

A **microblog** is a short blog post (sometimes sent from a mobile phone). Its appeal is that it's an immediate and portable way of communicating.

> **Twitter** is a service for people to communicate through the exchange of quick, frequent answers to one simple question: What are you doing?
>
> Users have 140 characters for each post – called a **tweet** – to say whatever they wish. Many tweets answer this question, but others could be responses to other tweets, links to webpages a user found interesting, musings, or questions.
> http://twitter.com/

Beautiful and beastly blogs

A **tumblelog** (or tlog) is a form of blog favouring short-form, mixed-media posts. Unlike blogs, tlogs are frequently used to share the author's creations, discoveries or experiences while providing little or no commentary.

Blogs vs. discussion forums

A blog is a more advanced way of communicating than a discussion forum as it offers personal ownership of posts – a place to use as an opinion column rather than a shared space for discussion.

The use of links within a blog allows for knowledge to be given context by linking quickly to it.

The frequency of update is designed around regular visits – highlighted by the reverse order of posting – unlike a discussion forum where an argument is usually worked through from first to last post.

You and a blog

Have you got a blog?

If YES: Think about how you have used it and what problems and rewards it has provided.

- Was it as easy to use as people said?
- Do you get many **comments** from other people?
- Is it difficult to have to continually update it with new posts?

If NO: Visit the edublogs site – http://edublogs.org/students/

Create an account (follow the instructions) and post an entry concerning what you have read in this section.

Don't panic! Take your time and breathe deeply (there's really nothing to it).

Blog positives

As a student, you might use a blog to share experiences, improve group communication, keep track of research, help your writing and for personal reflection and exploration of theories.

Sharing experiences

Blogs are great for mutual support as they allow you to share experiences with other students. You can get to know each other by reading and replying to each other's blogs without worrying about having to speak up in class (which can sometimes be intimidating).

Improving group communication

Blogs allow work to be shared with other group members by keeping them up to date about progress on a group project or allowing you and your tutor to provide group feedback. You can:

- conveniently access your blog anywhere and respond quickly
- interact to guide group members to address particular issues
- look at all individual blogs for a group and gain a broader picture or highlight particular issues.

Keeping track of research

Blogs are really useful as a way of maintaining a research diary – a place to store ideas, links and references.

A blog could help you to focus your research more effectively with the search facility letting you find ideas posted and making it easy to connect and track related material online over a sustained period of time.

Improving writing

Blogs can positively help with the development of a writing style. By writing every day for an audience – making sure your arguments are clear and concise – a blog might help your writing style and allow you to write in a more accessible, informal way.

It is worth noting that writing blogs is not for everyone so don't worry if you think that this is not going to work for you.

Personal reflection and a Personal Learning Environment (PLE)

Blogs are especially useful for reflective writing, allowing bloggers to gain insights into their thoughts at a particular moment for a deeper reflection of an experience.

You could use your blog entries as records and summaries of your activities over a period of time. You could then revisit the entries at a later date and reflect upon them: what you have done, what you have learnt and the successes or failures you might have experienced.

Exploration and accountability for theories

Blogs allow you to explore links between your own experiences and the theories you might study on your course.

If someone comments negatively on an idea you might have posted on your blog you need to respond to it, which could provide an excellent opportunity for proving your argument.

Blog negatives

Inaccurate and biased information

When visiting a blog you might view it as factual and authoritative, when in fact it is just like listening to someone on a soapbox.

Unlike discussion forums, blogs are unmediated and therefore offer a different place for expressing attitudes, opinions and ideas.

Blogs and universities

It can sometimes be seen as inappropriate for a blog to be hosted by an educational institution. For example, a UK university recently stopped hosting blogs maintained by academic staff, following problems with links to controversial content. New guidelines introduced by the university said that staff sites must be relevant to academic or administrative work.

Therefore, some universities prefer to use blogs located within password-protected VLEs, which mean people from outside the university are unable to view them.

Intellectual property

If a blog hosted within an educational institution includes content used without correct attribution then copyright is infringed. For example, a US university hosting student blogs contained one where a student had posted internal memos from a company suggesting their machines faced problems. The company threatened legal action against the student and the university.

Similarly, their open nature make blogs easy to copy and use elsewhere so you might be wary of sharing fledgling ideas – you might see your personal theories reproduced elsewhere before publication.

Blogs can date ideas so posting them could be seen as putting down a marker confirming someone had come up with an idea first. However, this can be a problem on systems where posts can be dated retrospectively (e.g. you could post an entry on 25 April 2009 but set the date so that it looks as if it was published on 13 January 2009).

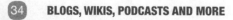

Communication and netiquette – blog tips

- A short, interesting title grabs attention.
- Try to make some aspect of your blog unique in terms of your post.
- Never use someone else's content without crediting them.
- Think before you post. As with email you don't want to post something you'll end up regretting – you might be writing for your future employer.
- Don't mix up topics – keep each post on one topic. If you want to talk about two different ideas write two different posts.
- If you read something interesting online and write about it, post a link to what you've been talking about.
- Be conversational in tone.
- It's polite to reply to comments about your posts.
- You don't need to start each post with a greeting like 'Dear Blog' or use your name at the end, as it will be automatically stamped with your user ID.
- Post regularly to ensure your readers keep coming back.
- Don't forget to include an author biography so that people reading know who you are.
- Make sure that your most popular posts are kept near the top of your blog so that they don't become difficult to find.

5 Wonderful and woeful wikis

What is a wiki?

A wiki is a group of webpages that allows users to add content but which also permits others (sometimes without restriction) to edit that content.

> **Wiki origins**
> The wiki term originates from the Hawaiian word for 'quick'.

Wikis vs. blogs

A blog shares writing and content in the form of posts and comments. While posting or commenting is open to members of a blog, no one can change a comment or post made by someone else. The usual format is: blog post – blog comment – blog comment. For this reason, blogs are often chosen to express individual opinions.

A wiki has a more open structure and allows others to change what anyone has written. This openness can overwrite individual opinion with group consensus. Unlike blogs, which are usually organised chronologically, wikis could initially be organised by links to other pages and then, at a later date, by the categories or concepts which emerge from the content.

BLOGS, WIKIS, PODCASTS AND MORE

Wiki characteristics

Wikis are simple to use, which makes creating content really easy. You usually only need to know a few basic commands, so, if you can use a word-processing package, a wiki should be just as easy to get to grips with.

Anyone is allowed to change anything on a wiki. They encourage collaborative working as they are designed for quick and easy revision with permissions and passwords not always required.

Wiki pages are in a constant state of flux. A page can have many different contributors, and copying content between pages – essentially plagiarism – is often acceptable (although references should always be attributed or acknowledged).

Wiki entries are often left unfinished (including mistakes) with users hoping that some-one will come along to complete the gaps or amend the text later on.

Each individual version of a wiki page (known as a revision) is saved to an online da-tabase. Wiki entries can be altered by reverting to a different version of the page (by using the **revision history**).

Wiki page titles are often combined into one word (e.g. History_of_Wikis or Oxford_English_Dictionary) to allow for quick, easy creation and linking of pages.

An example revision history:

Visit http://en.wikipedia.org/w/index.php?title=Oxford_English_ Dictionary&action=history to see the revision history for the Wikipedia page on the *Oxford English Dictionary*.

Why not compare two different versions to see what changes have been made?

You and a wiki

Do you already use a wiki socially or are you already using one on your course?

If YES: Think about how you have used it and what problems and rewards it has provided.

- Was it as easy to use as people said?
- Did you use it with other people?
- Was it frustrating seeing someone else amend your work without your being able to stop them?

If NO: Visit Wikipedia – http://en.Wikipedia.org

Pick an entry (a subject of interest or a band or TV programme you like). Create an account and make some changes to the article (maybe amending some information which is incorrect or missing).

or

Pick an entry (a subject of interest or a band or TV programme you like). Check the revision history by clicking on the History tab and compare some changes to see how the page has evolved.

You should now have a feel for what a wiki is and how you can use it.

Wiki positives

As a student, you might use a wiki to collect data, develop and review a project, track group work, do presentations, or create content or a review database.

Collecting data

A wiki can be very useful for collecting data from groups of people because it's easy to edit and allows multiple access. For example, students asked to collect data from peers using questionnaires could input the data directly onto a wiki page instead of emailing the information to an administrator. This has the twin benefits of saving time and eliminating potential administrative errors.

Developing and reviewing a project

A wiki makes it easy for you to write, revise and submit assignments, since all three activities can take place within one place. You could be given a wiki to develop an essay, and start tracking your research. This allows your tutor (or other students) to see what you are using, help you if you start to go off track, suggest other useful resources, or even obtain ideas for themselves.

You could draft your essay in a wiki, using the revision history to keep track of changes. This allows your audience to see your essay evolve over time, and continually comment on it. The wiki might also become the piece of work and format that you are assessed on.

Tracking group work and changes

Often student groups need to collaborate on an assignment and email different versions to each other with one person coordinating. This can cause problems – such as when two people think of the same idea and include it in different ways or when one group member misses a deadline.

Using a wiki allows a group to build and edit a document collaboratively whilst also making possible simple tracking as all members have immediate, equal access to the most recent version.

Group members can track research and ideas from anywhere they have internet access. Everyone can see what sources others have already checked and people with similar ideas can see and build on each other's work rather than duplicating it.

Making presentations

You can use wikis for presentations, instead of using software like Keynote or Power-Point. Your presentation will be available for access over the web immediately and you will be able to view it from any computer with internet access.

Also, you don't need to buy or use any special software to access your presentation.

Creating content

If you are asked to create a website for a project, a wiki is easy to use and allows you to add pages and design a simple navigation structure.

You can concentrate on developing content, instead of learning how to make a website.

Creating a review database

In the same way that Trip Advisor – http://www.tripadvisor.co.uk/ – allows users to comment on hotels they have stayed in, wikis allow a collaborative review database to be created.

For example, ten students could add their different reviews of a journal article they had read. Students could then see ten different views on what the article was about, how well it was written and the relevance it had to the subject area being studied.

Communication and netiquette – wiki tips

▸ Unless there is strong evidence to the contrary, assume that people who are working on a wiki are trying to help and not hurt it.

▸ Don't deliberately amend or suggest articles for deletion; there's no need to push rules to their limits or create work for other people just to prove a point.

▸ Contributors have different views and backgrounds, sometimes varying widely. Treating others with respect is the key to collaborating effectively.

▸ Some contributors might lack knowledge about wiki policies so always understand and be tolerant of them.

▸ Take care when using words or images that might be considered offensive or obscene by other users.

▸ When writing, remember that a wiki is not a blog, web space provider, or social networking site.

▸ **Edit warring** occurs when people repeatedly revert content edits to a page or subject area. Such behaviour is considered a breach of 'wikiquette', as it is an attempt to win a content dispute through brute force.

▸ Wikis work best when people with opposing opinions work together to find common ground. The 'Neutral Point of View' (**NPOV**) principle advises that all significant views can and should be documented proportionally.

More useful tips

Wikipedia has a resource section on good wiki practice:
http://en.Wikipedia.org/Wiki/Wikipedia:Policies_and_guidelines#Guidelines

Global wikis

Wikipedia

Wikipedia is a free encyclopaedia collaboratively written by users who are constantly striving to improve it by continuously making changes, all of which are recorded:
http://en.Wikipedia.org

If new material is added, it requests that you provide references. Facts that are unreferenced are routinely removed (although not immediately). It is a huge resource but not everybody who uses it realises that:

> *Anyone* in the world can edit almost any page.
> Often there is conflict between users about whether something is NPOV – Neutral Point of View – which is a fundamental Wikipedia principle.

In theory, users correct errors in Wikipedia until each article approaches perfection. Like other wikis, Wikipedia keeps a record of all changes made, so vandalism or incorrect information can be reversed – either automatically by the software, or by users who watch pages they are interested in.

Wikipedia also allows you to:

- click the history tab to see the most recent 50 changes
- pick two entries and select 'compare selected versions' to get a comparison of pages
- see if there is disputed content or a continuous editing and revision of content by people following particular agendas.

Wikipedia as a research tool (or not)

Wikipedia now has almost 10 million articles written in 253 languages (just under a quarter of which are in English). It is great for providing quick guides to subjects but remember that it's always a work in progress. For serious research, it can be a starting point but should not be viewed as the end point.

Use Wikipedia's notes, references and external links but *be cautious*.

Wikipedia and universities

Many universities question the reliability of information posted on Wikipedia:

- Marketing officials regularly monitor information because it can affect a university's reputation.

Wonderful and woeful wikis 45

- In 2007, a history faculty in the UK voted to ban undergraduates from citing Wikipedia.
- There is a concern about the wide variation in quality of Wikipedia articles, some of which include errors and examples of strange decisions.

You may be told, 'Don't use Wikipedia', for your essays but there is still a time and a place when it might be useful to look at. For example, if there is a term that you know nothing about (maybe an economic term like 'macroeconomics') Wikipedia is a good place to start: http://en.wikipedia.org/wiki/Macroeconomics

Then, by looking at the notes, references and external links on the page you can find some suggested places to go and find out more information – this would point you in the direction of works by Ragnar Frisch, John Maynard Keynes and Milton Friedman, amongst others. But you then need to go and read these to get a good detailed understanding of the term.

You shouldn't be taking what is written on Wikipedia as the gospel truth but as long as you are aware of its limitations and are well informed about how to use it then you will be OK. So do use it as a starting point but don't rely on it as evidence.

Think of it as if you're going to purchase a new jacket – you don't buy it from the first place you go to because you might get a better one somewhere else. So you do some checking first.

Citizendium

Citizendium is a 'citizens' compendium of everything' – an open wiki project aimed at creating an enormous, free and reliable encyclopaedia.

The project, started by a founder of Wikipedia, aims to improve on the Wikipedia model by adding gentle expert oversight and requiring contributors to use their real names. They hold over 7600 articles and have hundreds of contributors.
http://en.citizendium.org

Eduzendium

Eduzendium is a programme in which Citizendium partners with university programmes throughout the world to create high-quality, English-language entries for Citizendium.

The Eduzendium project allows students to write their assignments online on Citizendium on a given topic allocated by their tutor.
http://en.citizendium.org/Wiki/CZ:Eduzendium

Digital Universe

The vision of the Digital Universe is to organise the sum total of human knowledge and make it available to everyone. It is a growing collection of commercial-free portals mapping the highest-quality internet destinations, as recommended by experts.

Digital Universe might be of interest if you are studying or have an interest in the areas of Biodiversity, Climate Change, Energy, Environmental Health, Globalisation, Marine Ecology, or Pollution.

http://www.digitaluniverse.net/

Knol

Launched at the end of July 2008, Knol is a new service from Google which is intended as a repository of knowledge for everything from literature to DIY.

http://knol.google.com

Wiki negatives

Anyone can change anything

The main problem with wikis (like Wikipedia) is that there is no way of telling if anything you read on it is true or false.

Allowing anyone to edit content carries the risk of vandalism, inappropriate language, spam, and incorrect or inappropriate or copyright-protected content being published. This is both time-consuming and personally intensive to monitor.

As a result, many wikis require authorisation so that only registered members can modify content. However, this is no guarantee of security as registered users can then amend data to include incorrect information.

Wikipedia vandalism examples:

▶ US journalist John Siegenthaler wrote an article about the libellous material in his Wikipedia biography. The material was later revealed to have been a prank by someone who thought Wikipedia was a joke site.

▶ Immediately after England were knocked out of the 2006 World Cup by Portugal, entries for the players (specifically Cristiano Ronaldo) and manager were vandalised.

Structural problems

Another problem is with the organisation of pages in a wiki. Since a group rather than an individual essentially creates a wiki, structuring initial content for easy access can be challenging.

Working out the best approach for accessing and organising information on a wiki, and navigating the site and creating links to additional information needs to be addressed early and continuously monitored.

If not organised properly, wiki information can get out of control with pages not available to view or the same information being duplicated.

Wonderful and woeful wikis 49

Double trouble

Some wikis have no page locking system, so if two people edit the same page simultaneously, one set of changes will be not be captured.

Group mentality

A wiki represents the collective perspective of the group that uses it so it is possible for a wiki to have a collaborative bias. Over time, the values, perspectives and opinions of its users become embedded within it, so although they might seem well suited to reflecting current thoughts, wikis in fact reflect the perspectives of the group that writes them – especially on rapidly evolving topics or controversial issues.

Bias on Wikipedia

Some pages on Wikipedia dealing with controversial topics such as abortion or religious perspectives may show signs of disputed content. This could be a continuous editing and revisioning of content by people following particular agendas.

You can spot this by:
▸ Selecting the discussion tab, which allows users to suggest improvements or disagree with other user recommendations: http://en.Wikipedia.org/Wiki/Talk:Abortion

- Viewing the revision history. These links will help you to evaluate and make an informed judgement on the information you see: http://en.Wikipedia.org/w/index.php?title=Abortion&action=history

What is a podcast?

A podcast is an audio file that can be downloaded from a web source onto your computer, MP3 player or mobile phone.

Lecturers may sometimes provide parts or the whole of a lecture as a podcast for you to access. You can listen to it when and where you like, and as many times as you wish in order to fully understand and remember the information.

Podcasts can be accessed from an online repository like iTunes which enables them to be downloaded and played on an iPod. They can also be accessed on your VLE or from other websites.

To listen to them through your computer you can use your mouse to left-click onto the MP3 or **WMA** link supplied on a website and then save them to your computer.

To download a file, right-click, select 'Save as' and specify the destination to which you would like to save the file on your own computer.

Files can then be copied over to your MP3 player, mobile phone or your iPod.

Podcasting as learning software

TextHelp Systems produce Read&Write Gold, which has the ability to convert any text that you select and turn it into a sound file. You can listen to it later in the car, on the move or at home and it's simple to use.
http://www.texthelp.com/page.asp

Free online podcasts

▶ **Study skills:** Palgrave Macmillan provide you with podcasts for getting the most out of both your academic and personal life at university:
http://www.palgrave.com/skills4study/mp3s.asp

▶ **Subject specific: Audio Darwin**: The University of Cambridge has published the complete works of Charles Darwin online. MP3 versions are also available:
http://darwin-online.org.uk/audio_darwin.html

What is a vodcast?

A **vodcast** (or video podcast) is an audio-visual file that can be downloaded from a web source onto your computer, MP3 player or mobile phone.

Free online vodcasts

▶ **TED**: TED stands for Technology, Entertainment, Design. It started out as a conference bringing people together from those three worlds but since then its scope has widened.
http://www.ted.com/

▶ **iTunes U**: iTunes U makes the iTunes Store available for colleges and universities, enabling users to search, download and play course content just as they do with music. A growing number of US and UK universities are now distributing lectures through iTunes U.

iTunes U

In June 2008, iTunes U was opened to UK higher education facilities with University College London, the Open University and Trinity College Dublin all putting their lectures onto it. In October 2008, Oxford University and Cambridge University made lectures by leading academics available. Cambridge said it would bring the work of its Nobel Prize-winning academics within reach of a much wider audience, whilst Oxford said it would publish 150 hours of video and audio material of lectures and ideas from world-leading thinkers.

Initial offerings from UCL include material about neuroscience; the university's lunch-time lectures and an audio news round-up. The Open University is promising to make available 300 audio and video files with material from current courses. Trinity College Dublin is promising lectures from journalists, scientists, authors and politicians. http://www.apple.com/uk/education/itunesu_mobilelearning/itunesu.html

How to podcast

There are three steps to producing a podcast: *planning*, *recording* and *publishing*.

Podcast checklist:

Planning	Recording	Publishing
1 Plan what you want to talk about.	4 Rehearse once and record.	8 Publish your podcast.
2 Write some notes or key points for guidance.	5 Listen back to your recording and make adjustments.	
3 Rehearse once without recording.	6 Final recording.	
	7 Edit as required.	

Planning

Be professional and prepare. Unless you can remember everything off the top of your head, you need to have some notes written down before you start to record. This will make you sound more natural and it will also ensure you don't forget items or get lost in the middle of speaking. If you are recording a podcast with someone else, make notes on when each of you is going to speak to ensure confusion is kept to a minimum.

Rehearse your podcast once without recording it, to get a feel for timing and your subject. Have an idea of how long you want your podcast to be and check for timings during the recording to ensure you aren't running under or over time.

Recording

> **Audacity**
> Audacity is a free, easy-to-use audio editor and recorder which can be used for creating podcasts. Editing is simple and you can remove background noise or add sound effects to your podcast:
> http://audacity.sourceforge.net/

You need to have access to something to record your podcast on. This could be a mobile phone, a digital recorder or a computer. If you have a computer it will probably have an external microphone already, although you can buy a microphone to attach to the line-in socket of your computer if you want a slightly clearer sound.

On the second run-through, record your podcast. It will sound clearer if you limit the noise that is picked up by the microphone – background noise can be distracting – so try to find a quiet room.

Once you're satisfied that the podcast sounds OK, you're ready to record it for real. Don't worry if you make mistakes or if there are lots of 'ums' and 'errs' in it as these can be edited out to make it sound more professional using an editing/recording product like Audacity.

Once recorded, you will have a sound file containing your podcast. This will probably be in MP3, **WMA**, or **WMV** format (the same formats as the music files that you might listen to on your computer).

Listen back to this version and make any adjustments to notes and timings as required or make edits using Audacity.

Publishing

Once recorded, you will need to publish your podcast somewhere. Your tutor might ask you to upload it onto the VLE or, alternatively, you could post it to your blog, a wiki, a social networking site or even iTunes.

Get podcasting

A more in-depth guide to podcasting:

http://www.how-to-Podcast-tutorial.com/

Publicising your podcast

If you want to publicise your podcast you can submit it to iTunes where it will be globally accessible. Apple also have a range of useful resources on podcasting:

http://www.apple.com/itunes/store/Podcasts.html

What is RSS? Really Simple Syndication

News feeds allow you to see when websites or blogs have added new content. The feeds themselves are just webpages designed to be read by computers rather than people.

Like the internet, feeds cover almost any topic including education and entertainment. So if you found a site or blog relating to your subject interest you could receive regular updates via your feed.

Journal and magazine RSS feeds

Some journals, like the *British Journal of Educational Technology*, allow you to sub-scribe to a feed of new articles being published:
http://www.blackwellpublishing.com/journal.asp?ref=0007-1013

Feeds from magazines like *Wired* and the *New Scientist* allow you see when new stories of interest to you are published:
Wired feeds: http://www.wired.com/services/rss/
New Scientist feeds: http://www.newscientist.com/feed/feeds

How do I use RSS?

To use RSS you need a news reader – software that checks feeds and lets you read any new articles that have been added. Browser-based news readers let you view RSS feeds from any computer, whereas downloadable applications let you store them on your computer (in the same way that you either access your email at home or view it from a web-based service like Gmail).

> **Free news readers**
> Google Reader: http://www.google.com/intl/en/googlereader/tour.html
> NewsGator: http://www.newsgator.com/ngs/default.aspx

Most web browsers – like Firefox – contain a news reader. Some also automatically check for feeds for you when you visit a website, and display an icon when they find one. This can make subscribing easier.

Subscribing to a feed

Once you have chosen a news reader you need to decide what content you want to receive. If you click on the RSS button on a website you subscribe to the feed either by dragging the URL into your news reader or by copying the URL into a new feed.

Some feeds may just have a normal web link but most sites use an orange button marked as RSS:

RSS feed

Once you have subscribed, the feed links are displayed in your browser just like web-page links – you just click on a link to access it.

The art of searching, finding and assessing information

What do you need to know?

Searching for information is an essential part of studying. Wherever you are working, you will want to make sensible decisions so that you make the task of identifying and searching for information easier and quicker for yourself.

Information is all around us, and it can be worrying deciding where to start and what to use. Identifying the types of information you need will help you to choose which resources to use.

> **What sort of information do you need?**
> Ask yourself some questions about *why* you need the information, *what types* and *how much* you need.

What are you looking for?

Think about what you need to find out and use the source that best meets your requirements.

If you need ...	... start with/try
Current information	Newspapers and the internet (e.g. BBC) are the best places to look.
A brief summary or definition	Encyclopaedias, subject dictionaries or the internet (e.g. Wikipedia) are great starting points.
Practitioner information or research	Professional hard copy or online journals are good options.
Academic information or research	Textbooks, journals and bibliographic databases are good choices.

Whatever the purpose of finding information ...

- Choose a variety of sources of information, physical and electronic.
- Find and demonstrate different points of view through the selection of different sources.
- Don't rely too heavily on one source as it can present biased and unbalanced analysis, or might be too general.

The art of searching, finding and assessing information 63

▶ Follow the reference trail – academic articles contain a list of references directing you to relevant and sometimes useful work. This can lead you to information you might not have found in a traditional search.

Google definition

To see a definition in Google, type the word 'define' followed by a space and the word you want defined. Google will retrieve and display the definition at the top of your search results:

define World Wide Web

You can also get a list of definitions by using 'define:' with no space between it and the word or term you want defined:

define:World Wide Web

Searching for information

There are different approaches to looking for information, such as browsing and searching.

▶ **Browsing**: Useful when you want to explore what is available. It involves skimming through resources for possible leads or insights into useful information.
▶ **Searching**: Useful when you know what you are looking for. It involves selecting keywords for use with search tools in order to find relevant information.

Effective searching

1 **Analyse your topic**: Start by writing down your topic and thinking about the various search terms you could use to look for it (e.g. biodiversity, species, diversity).

2 **Devise a search strategy**: Identify exactly what kind of information you need and work out where the best place to find it will be (e.g. a definition of the term, what area you are interested in or how it is measured).

3 **Use appropriate search tools**: If you are searching for your topic in your university library you will probably want to use the library catalogue. If you are searching for information on the internet, you will want to use search engines, web directories and subject gateways. If you are looking for journal articles you will want to use bibliographic databases.

4 **Review your search strategy**: If your initial search does not help you find what you're looking for, consider other search terms and alternative search tools (e.g. biological, diversity, genetic, variation, conservation, biology).

5 **Record your results**: Make sure you note down the full details of any references you find. This makes it much easier to refer back to them when you are compiling evidence for a piece of work. If you are working on the internet, you can bookmark the web addresses of useful sites for later use or use a web tool (see **CiteULike** later in this chapter).

Using internet search tools

Although you will find lots of information on the internet, it can be difficult to find good quality information. Remember, the internet is *not* a library.

A web browser gives you access to the internet but to find a specific webpage you need to search for it as you would when looking for a book in a library or a file in an office drawer. If you know the URL you can access the page directly or alternatively you can use internet search tools such as search engines, web directories and subject gateways.

Search engines

Search engines let you look for information by typing keywords or search terms. They use software to scan the internet automatically and list what they find. Examples of this type of search tool are Google, Live Search, Wolfram Alpha and Cuil.

Pros:
▶ Very easy to use and quick.
▶ A great place to start a search.

Cons:
▶ Too much information is available to process so it's difficult to refine your search.

▸ Search engines are not library catalogues so information might be difficult to verify in terms of quality, authorship and date.

Google

Google is currently the most popular search engine and some browsers (like Firefox) come with it preinstalled. Google ranks its search page results via the popularity and number of links and hits to that site:
http://www.google.co.uk/

Live Search

Live Search is the name of Microsoft's web search engine. You can:
▸ view additional search results on the same web page
▸ adjust the amount of information displayed for each search result
▸ save searches and see them updated automatically.
http://www.live.com/

Cuil

Former workers at Google launched a new search engine called Cuil at the end of July 2008. Cuil claims it does a better and more comprehensive job of indexing information

online than any other search engine. However, it is too early to tell whether it will be as popular as other existing search engines.
http://www.cuil.com

Wolfram Alpha

A new search engine launching in May 2009, which aims to understand and answer questions – not just retrieve documents. http://www.wolframalpha.com

Don't be lazy!

- Don't be tempted to use just the first one or two links that Google returns when you search. Research suggests that 53.3% of searchers only look at the first or second link that Google returns (Arthur, 2006).
- Don't expect Google to provide all of the answers – try Google Scholar, Live Search or your library for links to e-journals and other online resources.
- Don't just rely on the internet: books, magazines, journals, radio and television can all provide you with help in tracking down interesting material which might be of use. Try to maintain a balance of access to print and electronic resources.

Web directories

Web directories let you browse websites arranged under different subject categories. They use real editors to decide what is included in lists and tend to cover popular subjects. They usually include a search option, so you can type in keywords like you do with search engines. An example of this type of search tool is the Yahoo! directory search.

Pros:

▶ More refined than a search engine so data quality will be better than a random search.

Cons:

▶ More time-consuming to use than a search engine.
▶ Sometimes difficult to navigate if you don't have a clear idea of what you are looking for.

Yahoo! directory search

This allows you to select terms to drill down and find specific content that you are interested in. For example:

    Health > Nutrition > Nutrients > Vitamins > Vitamin B12 *or*

    Arts & Humanities > Visual Arts > Graffiti > Magazines > Art Attack

http://search.yahoo.com/dir

The art of searching, finding and assessing information

Subject gateways

Subject gateways provide subject-focused sites selected and classified by subject specialists. Examples of this type of subject gateway are Intute and Copac.

Pros:

▶ Provide more targeted access to resources.
▶ Excellent quality and consistent materials.

Cons:

▶ More complex to use than a search engine.
▶ Not as intuitive and can be daunting if you don't know exactly what you are looking for.

Intute

Intute is a free online service providing you with access to the best resources for education and research:

http://www.intute.ac.uk/

Copac

Copac is a freely available library catalogue, giving access to the merged online catalogues of many UK and Irish academic and national libraries, as well as increasing numbers of specialist libraries:

http://copac.ac.uk/

Google Scholar

Google Scholar provides a simple way to search for academic literature. From one place, you can search across many disciplines and sources for peer-reviewed papers, theses, books, abstracts and articles:

http://scholar.google.co.uk/

It aims to sort articles the way researchers do, by considering the full text of each article, the author, the publication in which the article appears, and how often the piece has been cited in other literature. The most relevant results always appear on the first page.

What does it do?

Google Scholar allows you to:

- search diverse sources from one convenient place;
- find papers, abstracts and citations;
- locate a complete paper through your library or the web;
- learn about key papers in any area of research.

Searching using Google Scholar (1)

Searching by author

You can enter the author's name in quotations: "a smith". To increase the number of results, you can use initials rather than the full first name.

If you find too many papers that mention an author, you can try "author:" to search for specific authors. For example, you could try [author:smith], [author:"a smith"], or [author:"Arthur smith"].

Searching by title

You can put the paper's title in quotations: "Observational Evidence of Recent Change in the Northern High-Latitude Environment".

Google Scholar will automatically find the paper as well as other papers which mention it.

How do I find recent research?

Clicking on "Recent articles" on the right-hand side of the results page sorts your results to help you find newer research more quickly.

The ordering considers factors like the prominence of the author's and journal's previous papers, as well as the full text of each article and how often it has been cited.

Searching using Google Scholar (2)

What does the Related Articles link do?

For each search result, Google Scholar tries to determine which articles in the index are most closely related to it. You can see a list of these articles by clicking "Related Articles".

The list of related articles is ranked primarily by how similar these articles are to the original result, but also take into account the relevance of each paper.

Advanced searching techniques

Within the Advanced Search page you can specify keywords, which must appear in both the article and the publication name, or search for literature within seven distinct areas of research. This allows you to target your search for papers in specific publications or search by category.

Why are there author names at the bottom of the results page?

Google Scholar automatically suggests authors related to your query – you can click on an author's name and you'll see their papers. Finding authors who publish on the topics you're interested in is a useful method of discovering related work you may not have otherwise found.

More help

Visit the Help section of Google Scholar for more help on using it:
http://scholar.google.com/intl/en/scholar/help.html

Google Book Search

Google Book Search allows you to browse books online and if the book is out of copyright, or the publisher has given Google permission, you'll be able to see a preview of the book and in some cases the entire text.
http://books.google.co.uk/

If it's in the public domain and free of copyright then you can even download a **PDF** copy.

What does it do?

Each item includes an 'About this book' page with basic bibliographic data like title, author, publication date, length and subject.

For some books you may also see additional information like key terms and phrases, references to the book from scholarly publications or other books, chapter titles and a list of related books.

An example search using Google and Google Scholar

Original search query

I have developed a pilot DVD for students and need some help with some articles or information on developing such material. I have looked on the databases but have struggled to find articles specifically looking at the issues of making a DVD and using it as a teaching tool for nursing students.

Search strategy: Google

A general Google search using the term "using video supporting teaching" found one article of interest:

> Questioning, promoting and evaluating the use of **streaming** video to support student learning,
>
> K Shephard, *British Journal of Educational Technology*, 2003, Blackwell Synergy

Search strategy: Google Scholar

The article of interest is cited by three others in Google Scholar http://scholar.google.com/scholar?hl=en&lr=&cites=15732435944621216779
and has a number of articles relating to it: http://scholar.google.com/scholar?hl=en&lr=&q=related:CxS8OiPXVNoJ:scholar.google.com/

> The results of a Google Scholar search on recent articles about "using video to teach nursing" http://scholar.google.com/scholar?hl=en&lr=&scoring=r&q=using+video+to+teach+nursing&as_ylo=2002
>
> One for "interactive teaching nursing" http://scholar.google.com/scholar?hl=en&lr=&scoring=r&q=interactive+teaching+nursing&as_ylo=2002
>
> Finally, one for "dvd teaching nursing" http://scholar.google.com/scholar?hl=en&lr=&scoring=r&q=dvd+teaching+nursing&as_ylo=2002

Thinking out of the box

If your initial search does not help you to find what you're looking for, you may wish to try different search terms and alternative search tools.

Also, thinking out of the box can sometimes yield good results.

For example, if you have been looking for resources around the issue of "maternal bonding" but have had no success, why not try searching under "skin to skin contact" or even "baby cuddles".

Sometimes the most straightforward approach can get the best results!

Example: Water pollution in the UK
Search 1 (basic): "UK pollution coast sea rivers water"

Search 2 (advanced): "water quality environment sediment marine sustainable development"

Search 3 (targeted): "surfers against sewage pollution Cornwall"

Mapping/analysing information

Record keeping is important and not the same as making notes (which also has to happen), so it is a good idea to try developing a strategy to manage your search results and readings. This will help you to get the most from your material. There are various ways of doing this. None is right or wrong so try to find one that suits you.

> The key thing to remember when mapping information is to use a system which is easy to use and that works for YOU.

Web 2.0 literature review

Kate Hoskins recently started a PhD. Each week, she updates her evolving thesis on her wiki and adds a blog reflection to go with the update. She also invites comments on her literature review via her blog:

Evolving literature review wiki: http://litreview.pbwiki.com/
Blog reflections: http://onlinelitreview.blogspot.com/

Mapping with a wiki

Mapping via a wiki would mean that each page would consist of information on each approach with links to specific authors:

```
Home page
|
---------------- Theme #1
     |
          ---------------- Author #1
|
---------------- Theme #2
     |
          ---------------- Author #1
     |
          ---------------- Author #2
|
---------------- Theme #3
```

Mapping with a blog

You could map your information into separate blog posts for each item of literature in the order in which you read them or intend to present them. In each blog posting you could identify each item by its author and write a short précis of the themes, theories, models or approach:

Post 1: Theme #1 and author details

Post 2: Theme #2 and author details

Post 3: Theme #3 and author details

Referencing

Good practice

You need to include references in your work to support your research, provide evidence of your reading, avoid allegations of plagiarism and acknowledge the sources you have used. Consistency and accuracy are important to enable your reader to easily identify and locate the material to which you have referred.

Make sure you note down the full details of the references you find. This makes it much easier to refer back to them. If you are working on the internet, you can save the web addresses of useful sites as bookmarks, tag them on Delicious (see p. 82) or save them into CiteULike (see p. 85).

> **What is a reference?**
>
> A reference is information referring to material written by others whether directly quoted, paraphrased or summarised. References are cited within the text and are also included in the references section at the end of the text.
>
> The same set of rules should be followed every time you cite a reference.

How do I reference?

Your college or university will have a particular approach to referencing that they will want you to use. Your friendly library should be able to provide you with a handout or information containing the details of the particular referencing style that you will need to adopt.

The two main elements are the in-text reference and the references section.

In-text reference

This information in Harvard style (the most commonly used in UK universities) will include the author's surname, the year of publication and a page reference when you quote, summarise or paraphrase a specific section of work.

Examples of in-text references include:

▶ Smith and Jones (2009) have proposed that …
▶ A more recent study (Arthur, 2009) concluded that …

These citations then appear as full bibliographic references at the end of a piece of work.

Full reference in the references section

Information for books includes the author's surname and initials, followed by year of publication, then the title and edition (if not the first), then the place of publication and the publisher:

> SMITH, A.L. and JONES, C.G. 2009. *Principles of Information Literacy* (3rd edition). Manchester: Palgrave Macmillan.

Information for journal articles will include the author's surname and initials, followed by the year of publication, the title of the article, followed by the journal title, volume and issue number, and page numbers:

> ARTHUR, S. 2009. Information Literacy Report. *Journal of Information Literacy*, 15 (3), 155–159.

Delicious

Delicious is a social bookmarking website. Its primary use is to store bookmarks online, which allows you to access them from any computer and add bookmarks from anywhere, too. You can use Delicious to:

- keep bookmarks to favourite websites, articles and items of interest
- share websites with other students and the Delicious community
- discover new things.

You can organise your collection of bookmarks by using a system known as tagging. **Tags** are words used to describe what you are bookmarking (separated by a space) that you can assign to bookmarks on Delicious.

Tags function like keywords when you search for things, but you are also able to choose them for yourself. You can assign as many tags to a bookmark as you like and rename or delete them as and when you like.

A Delicious idea

Visit the Delicious site: http://delicious.com/

Read through the instructions and when you are ready register for an account. If you are happy with the instructions you can install buttons on your browser that make it quicker for you to tag via Delicious, but this is not a requirement.

You will shortly be tagging to your heart's content …

Mapping with tags

An example of tagging

If you saved an article on the environment, you could use these tags:

green article april2008 pollution ethical oilspill environment

You can use the tags that make the most sense to you. Tagging is really intuitive but can take some practice to fully understand, as there are no wrong or right tags. You can use tags to describe an article or website's subject, location, name, category, or ideas – anything you can think of could be a tag.

As everybody tags, you begin to build a collaborative library of related information. To see everybody's Delicious bookmarks about the environment visit: http://delicious.com/tag/environment

Let's get ready to tag

After registering on Delicious, tag the following four sites:

http://en.Wikipedia.org/Wiki/Main_Page

http://en.citizendium.org/Wiki/Main_Page

http://scholar.google.co.uk/

http://www.intute.ac.uk/

When saving or editing a bookmark, there are fields for Title, URL, Notes and Tags.

In the **Title** field select a title meaningful to you or leave it as it is. The **URL** field will already be filled in for you so doesn't need changing. In the **Notes** field write a brief description of the site to help you remember it (this could be some text from the webpage you are tagging). In the **Tag** field, enter as many tags as you like, each separated by a space.

You may notice lists of tags underneath the form. 'Popular tags' are what other people have tagged this page as, and 'recommended tags' are a combination of tags you have already used and tags that other people have used. You are under no obligation to use any of these. Think about what tags or words would help you to remember this page a few years from now.

When you have finished, visit your Delicious site again and you should see four items showing on your page. Compare them to the completed page below and see which different tags you selected. If you think there are other tags that you want to add or remove then just select 'edit' by the side of the item and add or delete as required.

Wiki activity comparison:
Visit http://delicious.com/andybook and compare your completed page with it. Does it look very similar? How many different tags did you use – have you missed out any tags that might have been useful?

CiteULike

CiteULike is a free service that helps you store, organise and share academic papers you are reading. When you see a paper on the web that interests you, you can click one button and have it added to your personal library.

CiteULike automatically extracts citation details, so there's no need to type them in yourself. It works from within a web browser so you don't need to install special software. Like Delicious, because your account is stored on a server, you can access it from any computer that has internet access.

CiteULike has a flexible filing system based on tags. You can choose whichever tags you want, and apply as many as you like to a paper. You can also use tags to group papers together.

Trying CiteULike

Visit the CiteULike site: http://www.citeulike.org/

Read through the instructions on registering for an account (click on the Register button on the top right-hand corner of the screen) and when you are ready, register for an account.

Once you have created an account select some articles of interest you have found by searching Google Scholar or go to the end of this book and complete the DIY Literature Review to find some articles.

Post and tag your articles using your account.

 BLOGS, WIKIS, PODCASTS AND MORE

The quality of information

The internet contains masses of information and you can find information on most topics if you know how to search effectively. However, the quality of the information found can be extremely variable.

When you select information in an academic library, books and journals have been evaluated for their usefulness and relevance. If you use the internet, you need to think carefully and be critical of the information you find.

Assessing quality

Kathy Schrock (2009) suggests five W's for evaluating a website:

WHO

▸ Who wrote the pages and are they an expert?

▸ Is a biography of the author included?

▸ How can you find out more about the author?

WHAT

▸ What does the author say is the purpose of the site?

▸ What else might the author have in mind for the site?

WHEN

▸ When was the site created?

▸ When was the site last updated?

WHERE

▸ Where does the information come from?

▸ Where can I look to find out more about the producer/sponsor?

WHY

▸ Why is this information useful for my purpose?

▸ Why should I use this information?

▸ Why is this page better than another?

How do you know that the information in this book is correct?

Luckily for you, this book has been reviewed by experts (an editor and a publisher) who have ensured that it is of a good quality (!).

In your studies, you need to approach all information that you encounter with a critical perspective. You should question the reliability of information you find and develop skills in deciding what might and might not be valid, taking care to look out for biased information, misinformation or propaganda.

Examples might include information based on personal anecdotes rather than independent published research; alternative therapies offered as cure-all remedies; or information that presents only one side of an argument.

You and an opinion blog
Locate an opinion blog on a green issue (such as Biofuels or the Environment) or use one of these:
Green Blog: http://green-blog.org
Greenpeace Weblogs: http://weblog.greenpeace.org/

Considering what you have just read, how can you ascertain whether the viewpoint in these blogs is accurate and unbiased?

Communicating information effectively

Like most activities, being able to express yourself clearly in writing is a skill, which can be practised and improved. You should aim to get your message across clearly, accurately and in a style appropriate to the context in which you are writing.

While studying, you will be required to write in a variety of styles. You may be writing email messages, blog and wiki entries, or longer and more complex types of writing like essays, reports, group projects or research papers. Your approach will depend on the purpose of the writing and the audience you are writing for.

Before you start writing, think about your aims:
‣ Why are you doing it?
‣ What is the purpose of your writing?
‣ Who is your target audience? (Who will be reading it?)
‣ What type of writing will you be doing?

Writing for online: draft

Be stylish: Is your review easy to read? Is the writing appropriate? Are all of your references included and written correctly? Does it make sense when you read it?

Use evidence: Your interpretation of sources must be backed up with evidence to show that what you are saying is valid. Are your own ideas and opinions clear to the reader? Are there sufficient examples and evidence to prove them?

Be selective: Select only the most important points in each source to highlight. The type of information you choose to mention should relate directly to your focus.

Be careful: Are the punctuation, spelling and grammar OK? Always use a spell checker if you have access to one and make sure the language setting is either English (UK) or English (US). If you don't have access to a spell checker, try using a dictionary for a second opinion.

Be yourself: While the literature review presents others' ideas, your voice should be the one that the reader hears when reading it.

Google Docs

If you don't have access to word processing software but do have a browser and an internet connection, you could try Google Docs. This is a free, web-based word processor and spreadsheet, which allows you to share and collaborate online.
http://docs.google.com

Writing for online: revising your draft

Once you've completed your first draft, check it over to make sure that it follows the specified objectives and outcomes. Most writers revise a draft many times before they are happy and writing is rarely perfect the first time around (especially with this book!!!). Here are some tips for revising:

Be concise: Rewrite your review so that you've presented your information in the most concise manner – get rid of waffle.

Take a break: Try to take regular breaks between drafts. It is easier to come back to writing fresh and you will be more likely to spot what needs altering.

Be critical: Get rid of unnecessary jargon or slang and don't be afraid to remove sections you don't feel are good enough or relevant (consider saving them in another document – they might come in useful at some point in the future elsewhere).

Be methodical: Double-check that you've documented your sources and formatted the review and references appropriately. Check once again for mistakes in typing, spelling and grammar.

Don't forget to treat yourself: Once you've finished the final draft, treat yourself. How about a cup of tea, a biscuit if you've worked hard, a chocolate biscuit if you've worked really hard, or a chocolate bar if you've worked incredibly hard! Treats are a good way of helping you as they encourage you to complete goals.

Be safe and back up

If you are writing online, always remember to save your progress every now and then as computer systems can crash and web browsers have a habit of freezing at just the wrong moment.

The art of searching, finding and assessing information

If you're writing a draft in Word before posting it to a discussion forum (a good idea in case the forum goes down when you're posting), always save at least once every 15 minutes. If you have the automatic save enabled then always check it is actually saving your work. Also, be careful and always take a bit of extra time reading messages that ask you if you want to save – one wrong button push can have disastrous effects.

Don't forget to take a back-up of your files in case of an accident or if something happens to your computer. For example, copy the latest version of your work to a portable USB memory stick so that in the event of a crisis you still have a copy of it to use (and if you lose your memory stick you will have the computer copy to fall back on). Alternatively, you could email a copy of your work to another email address as a further precaution.

8 The literature review process: a short but lovely overview

What is it?

The aim of a literature review is to show your reader that you have read, and have a good understanding of, the main published work concerning a question or topic. There is not enough room in this book to cover a full literature review so we will be looking at the first two stages of the process.

Stages of a literature review

1 Selecting a question for the review.
2 Searching for suitable research.
----
3 Sampling research to be reviewed.
4 Representing characteristics of the studies.
5 Analysing findings.
6 Interpreting results.
7 Writing the review.

Categories of literature

- **Primary** sources are written by the investigator.
- **Secondary** sources are written by someone other than the investigator.

Be aware of the difference between primary and secondary sources in your reading, especially in journal articles.

What is peer review?

Some journal articles will have been through review processes with editors and publishers before publication. A peer-reviewed paper has been independently scrutinised for its credibility by experts in the particular field before publication.

Some papers explicitly address issues of application by making recommendations or discussing the implications of the findings in relation to practice. Others will leave the evaluation up to the reader. By studying the paper in detail and reflecting on the conclusions you will be able to make an informed judgement on whether this is the case.

Types of literature

There are different types of literature that might be useful for a literature review:

Type	Can I find them online?
Journal articles ▸ Aimed at a specific audience ▸ Quicker to publication than books (the time elapsed between writing and publication is less) ▸ Usually peer-reviewed	Available as either hard copy or online (sometimes only online).
Books Subject-specific books are aimed at different audiences and pitched at different academic levels. Material published in books is usually more detailed in the development of arguments (depending on the individual book), provides a more extensive review of the literature and the subject, and offers a more comprehensive treatment of the subject area compared to journal articles. It is unlikely that recent research and development will be published in books.	Usually available in print and some are also online (sometimes e-books are only available online). However, the library is still the place for most of the books you will be expected to read.

Type	Can I find them online?
Official publications Policy documents published by government departments that usually provide information as well as government strategies, which relate to public services.	Can usually be found online.
Conference proceedings Conferences, seminars and workshops provide a space for critical appraisal of ongoing work.	Slides and **abstracts** can be found on conference websites, and proceedings might be published in hard copy or online in a journal or book of conference proceedings.
Systematic reviews Systematic reviews are written by practitioners and academics and seek to synthesise evidence on one topic by a tightly structured list of inclusion criteria, methods of analysis and evaluation. Especially useful for research students.	Available as either hard copy or online.

Type	Can I find them online?
Other sources ▸ Dissertations ▸ Edited collections and literature reviews ▸ Methodological and confessional writings	Available as either hard copy or online. Location will depend on the type of writing and the author (for example, some people might make their dissertation available on the web whilst others prefer not to do so).

DIY literature review: getting started

The following exercise might prove useful in getting you to start thinking about some of the early stages of the literature review process.

> **1 An idea**
>
> Remember that you do need to know what you're looking for before you can find it!
>
> Think about the area in which you are studying or working and see if you can think of an idea for a problem/question to be addressed, or pick from one of these:
>
> ▸ Climate change (e.g. *How is climate change affecting the North Pole?*)
> ▸ Business (e.g. *How can mobile phones be used as marketing tools?*)
> ▸ Health (e.g. *Is using computer software to assist with decision making a good idea?*)

2 The search

Thinking about your area of interest, spend some time searching the internet for some interesting articles that might be useful to read or make a note of.

Try a selection of different searches using the methods we have covered in this book to see how the results vary.

or

From our list in **1. An idea** use these terms:

▶ Climate change ("climate change north pole environment arctic")
▶ Business ("mobile phones marketing opportunities ad campaigns")
▶ Health ("computer software health decision making effects")

BLOGS, WIKIS, PODCASTS AND MORE

The end bit – coda

Not everything discussed in this book will be useful to you, and it might be that using some of these tools for study won't work for you. Even so, don't get depressed or frustrated or worry if you don't understand or can't use the suggestions in here.

Using the internet and computers for study skills is exactly the same as any other subject or hobby that you might have. The best way of improving in the areas that this book discusses (as with any area of your life) is by practice, practice and more practice.

Good luck with your studies and on your own personal technological study skill journey.

Andy

References

Arthur, C. 2006. Top of the Heap. Available from: http://www.guardian.co.uk/
technology/2006/aug/31/searchengines.Wikipedia (Accessed 2 April 2009)

Berners-Lee, T. 1999. *Weaving the Web: The Past, Present and Future of the World
Wide Web*. London: Orion Business.

CIFAS. 2009. Is Identity Theft Serious? Available from: http://www.cifas.org.uk/
default.asp?edit_id=561-56#Is_Identity_Theft_Serious_ (Accessed 2 April 2009)

CILIP. 2009. Information Literacy: Definition. Available from: http://www.cilip.org.uk/
policyadvocacy/learning/informationliteracy/definition/default.htm
(Accessed 2 April 2009)

OFCOM. 2009. Social Networking. Available from: http://www.ofcom.org.uk/advice/
media_literacy/medlitpub/medlitpubrss/socialnetworking/ (Accessed 2 April 2009)

Schrock, K. 2009. The Five W's of Web Site Evaluation. Available from:
http://kathyschrock.net/abceval/5ws.pdf (Accessed 2 April 2009)

SCONUL. 2009. The Seven Pillars of Information Literacy Model. Available from:
http://www.sconul.ac.uk/groups/information_literacy/seven_pillars.html
(Accessed 2 April 2009)

Shimmon, R. 2000. From Digital Divide to Digital Opportunity. Available from: http://www.unesco.org/webworld/points_of_views/shimmon.shtml (Accessed 2 April 2009)

Glossary

abstract A brief summary of a research article, thesis, review or conference proceeding. Often used to help the reader quickly understand the paper's purpose.

asynchronous communication Two-way communication that occurs with a time delay, allowing someone to respond when they like.

BCC (blind copy) If you send an email as a blind copy, recipients only see their own email address, not everybody you send it to.

blog (short for weblog) A blog is an online journal that is frequently updated and intended for general public consumption.

blogger A person who writes a blog.

browser A piece of software that allows you to view a webpage on the internet (e.g. Firefox and Internet Explorer).

CiteULike A free service, which helps you store, organise and share academic papers you are reading.

comment A response to a blog post.

discussion forum A place where messages are entered into a common discussion area. Forums enable electronic conversations to develop – users either post new messages or respond to existing ones.

discussion list A place where people with a common interest can communicate together. A discussion list enables one-to-many communication via email, for support, advice and sharing of experiences.

discussion thread A series of messages on a discussion forum between two or more people, which forms an archive of a discussion.

DNFTT (Do Not Feed The Troll) Ignore this attempt at irritation in a post or email.

edit war The opposite of NPOV on a wiki, with two or more sides each fighting to make their version of the wiki page the only one.

email (electronic mail) A computer-based communication system that allows users to send and receive messages asynchronously.

email address An email address determines the sender and recipient of a message in electronic communication (like your postal address).

flaming A flame could be sent/posted to insult or complain with the intention of causing offence or provoking a response.

hacking Illegally accessing other people's computer systems for destroying, disrupting or carrying out illegal activities.

identity fraud Finding personal details and using them to open bank accounts and get credit cards, loans, state benefits and documents such as passports and driving licences in your name.

instant messaging (IM) A form of real-time communication between two or more people based on typed text.

keywords These are words and phrases entered into a search engine to reach a result page.

linklog A collection of URLs that the owner considers interesting enough to collect. Unlike a blog, postings are limited to one link per posting and a title with a short description or comment.

malware (malicious software) A program or file designed to specifically damage or disrupt a system, such as a virus, worm or trojan horse.

microblog A short blog post (sometimes sent from a mobile phone) typically containing around 140 characters.

MPEG (Moving Picture Experts Group) A standard for compressing sound and movie files into an attractive format for downloading or streaming across the internet.

MP3 An audio file format, based on MPEG technology. It creates very small files suitable for streaming or downloading over the internet.

netiquette Network etiquette, the dos and don'ts of online communication.

NPOV (Neutral Point of View) Advises that all significant views can and should be documented proportionally on a wiki.

password A secret word or string of characters and numbers used to gain entry or access to information. A password is usually only known by the user and is used alongside a user ID.

PDF (Portable Document Format) A file format created by Adobe Systems for document exchange.

phishing Attempting to steal personal data by requesting information via electronic spoofing.

podcast An audio file that can be downloaded from a web source onto your computer, MP3 player or mobile phone.

post A blog or discussion forum entry.

revision history A historical log or record of changes made to a wiki page or project.

RSS (Really Simple Syndication) A method of sharing and broadcasting content such as news from a website. News feeds allow you to see when websites or blogs have added new content.

shouting Typing communication (like emails) in capitals.

social networking Social networking refers to websites or services that allow you to connect with friends, family and colleagues online, as well as meet people with similar interests or hobbies (e.g. Facebook, MySpace).

spamming The abuse of email to indiscriminately send unsolicited bulk messages.

spoofing Pretending to be someone else. The deliberate inducement of a user or a resource to take an incorrect action.

spyware (spying software) Software that is installed on a computer without the user's knowledge and transmits information about the user's computer activities over the internet.

streaming The transmission of digital audio or video, or the listening and viewing of such data without first storing it.

subject gateways Subject gateways provide subject-focused websites selected and classified by subject specialists (e.g. Intute and Copac).

tag A word used to describe what you are bookmarking or posting. Tags function like keywords and allow you to search for things.

tag cloud A collection of tags.

trojan horse A virus in which malicious or harmful code is contained inside apparently harmless programming or data.

trolling Posting with the intention of annoying someone or disrupting a discussion.

tumblelog (tlog) A form of blog favouring short-form, mixed media posts.

tweet A short post of up to 140 characters on the microblogging application Twitter.

twitter A microblogging application that is part blog, part social networking site and part instant messaging tool. It provides people with the ability to communicate through the exchange of quick, frequent answers to one question: What are you doing?

URL (Uniform Resource Locator) An address that specifies the location of a file on the internet (like your postal address).

user ID A person's identification, usually a string of characters and numbers relevant to the user (e.g. initial followed by surname: asmith) used to gain entry or access to information. A user ID is usually only known by the user and is used alongside a password.

virus A dangerous computer program with the characteristic feature of being able to generate copies of itself, and thereby spread.

VLE (Virtual Learning Environment) Provides a place to access different resources and materials that you might be expected to use on a course.

vodcast (video podcast) An audio-visual file that can be downloaded from a web source onto your computer, MP3 player or mobile phone.

Web 2.0 A second generation of web-based communities and services (such as social networking, wikis and blogs) that aim to help creativity, collaboration and sharing.

wiki A collection of website pages, each of which can be visited and edited by anyone.

Wikipedia A free content, multilingual encyclopaedia written collaboratively by contributors around the world.

WMA (Windows Media Audio) An audio file encoded for use with Windows Media Player. WMA files can be streamed or downloaded for playback.

WMV (Windows Media Video) The companion program to WMA, but for video and/or audio (instead of just audio). WMV files can be streamed or downloaded for playback.

worm A computer program which replicates itself and is self-propagating. Worms, as opposed to viruses, are meant to spawn in network environments.

WWW (World Wide Web) Another name for the internet.

Index

ALSO IN THE POCKET STUDY SKILLS SERIES

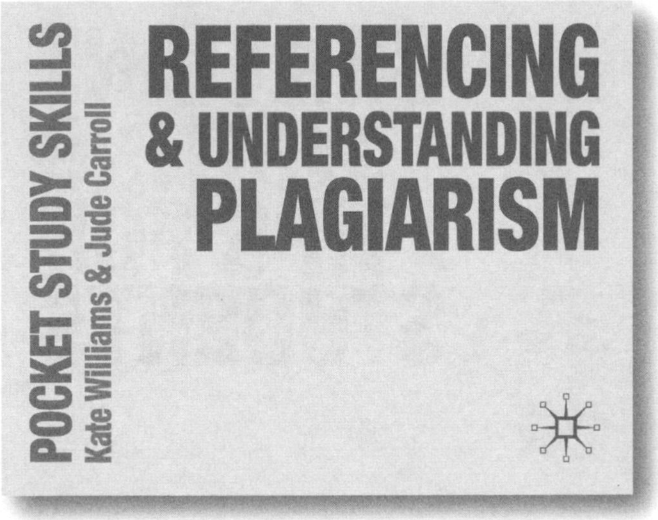

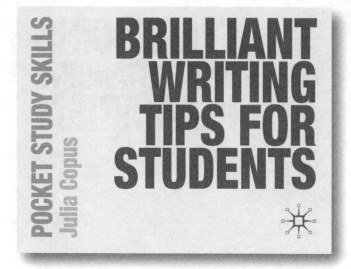

ALSO IN THE POCKET STUDY SKILLS SERIES

POCKET STUDY SKILLS

Julia Copus

BRILLIANT
WRITING
TIPS FOR
STUDENTS

POCKET STUDY SKILLS

Kate Williams

GETTING CRITICAL

POCKET STUDY SKILLS

Janet Godwin

PLANNING YOUR ESSAY

SCIENCE STUDY SKILLS

POCKET STUDY SKILLS

Sue Robbins